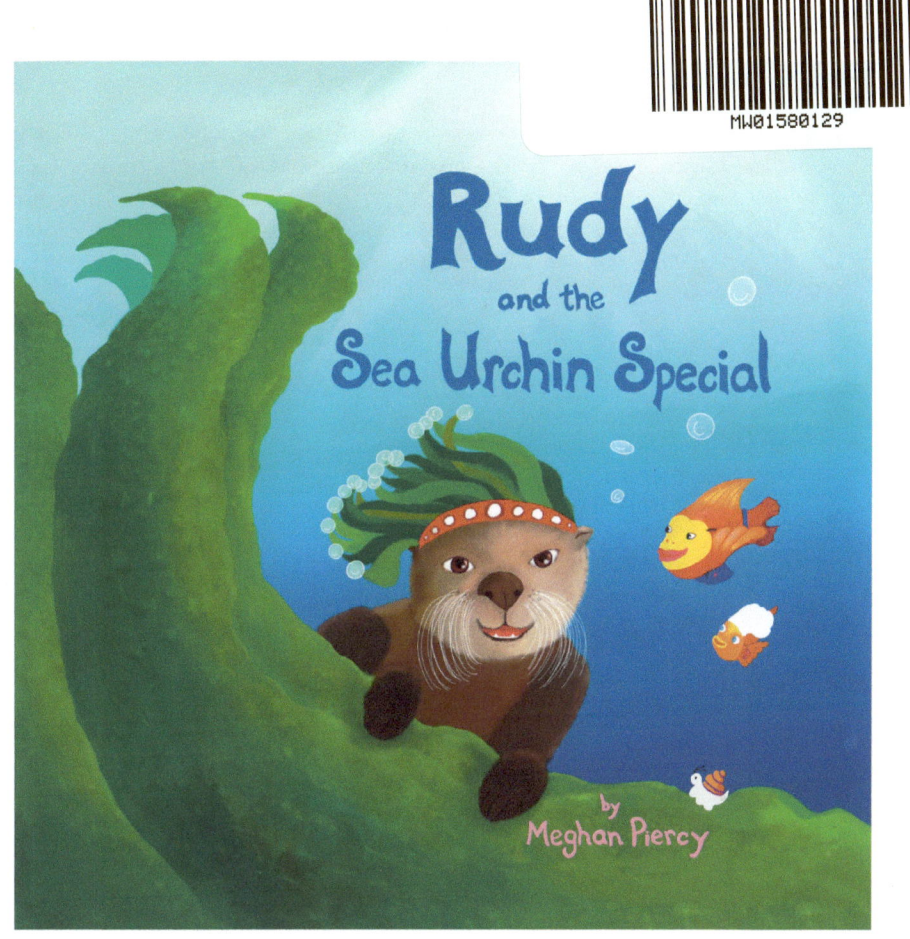

Blue Marble Friends, LLC
Nashua

Acknowledgements

I wish to express deep gratitude to my mother Bernice who instilled in me a love of nature and reading at a young age; to Stephen Mooser who helped usher this story into existence when I was a student at College of the Atlantic and for his periodic advice and encouragement along the way; to Marlo Garnsworthy at Icebird Studio for her deft editing with both text and illustration; and to Emma Wallace who made an important contribution to page nine when, at age six, she exclaimed, "And no Canopy Cafe!"

RUDY AND THE SEA URCHIN SPECIAL
Copyright 2022 by Meghan Piercy

All rights reserved. No part of this book may be reproduced, transmitted or stored in an information retrieval system in any form or by any means, graphic, electronic or mechanical, including photocopying, taping, and recording, without prior permission of the publisher, except in the case of brief quotations embodied in critical articles or reviews. Thank you for supporting the author/illustrator's hard work by purchasing an authorized copy of this book.

ISBN: 978-17367045-0-9 (hardcover)
ISBN: 978-17367045-1-6 (paperback)
ISBN: 978-17367045-2-3 (ebook)

Library of Congress Control Number: 2022905252

info@bluemarblefriends.com
www.bluemarblefriends.com

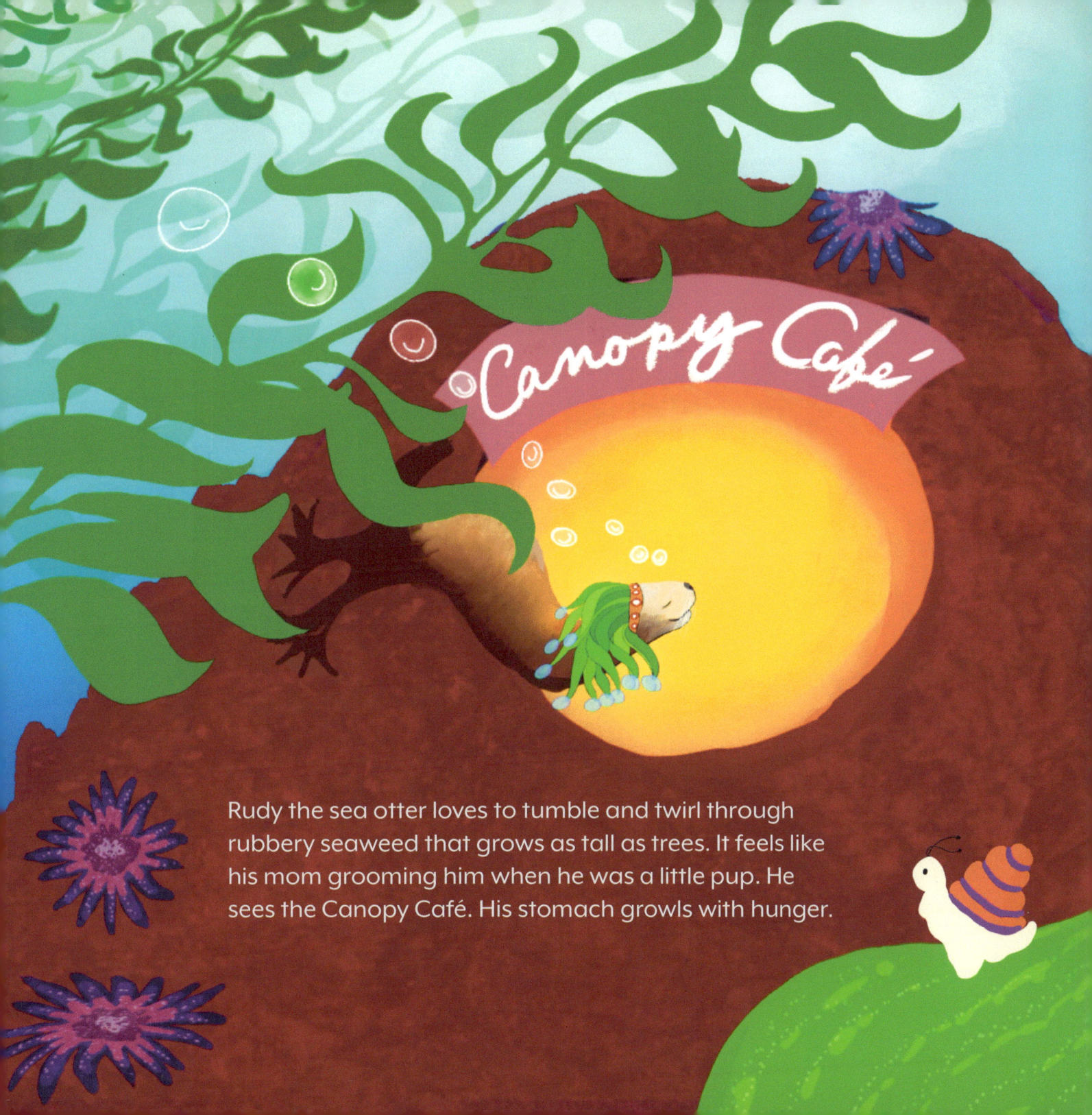

Rudy the sea otter loves to tumble and twirl through rubbery seaweed that grows as tall as trees. It feels like his mom grooming him when he was a little pup. He sees the Canopy Café. His stomach growls with hunger.

Rudy winks hello to Magda the eel, who chats with her book group about faraway places like Japan.

"Hiya, Scout!" he calls across the room to the server, who bustles about keeping the crowd well-fed.

But Rudy worries as he passes Dominic the shark. He's not sure if the shark is sneering or practicing his toothy grin.

Rudy sees Opal the snail but doesn't bother to say hello. She's too small, he thinks, to have much to say.

Scout dashes into the kitchen. Her squeaky voice floats through an open door.

"I'm glad Rudy eats so many urchins," she says to Ripples. "Without him, there would be so many they'd eat all the kelp in the forest! Without Rudy, we'd have..."

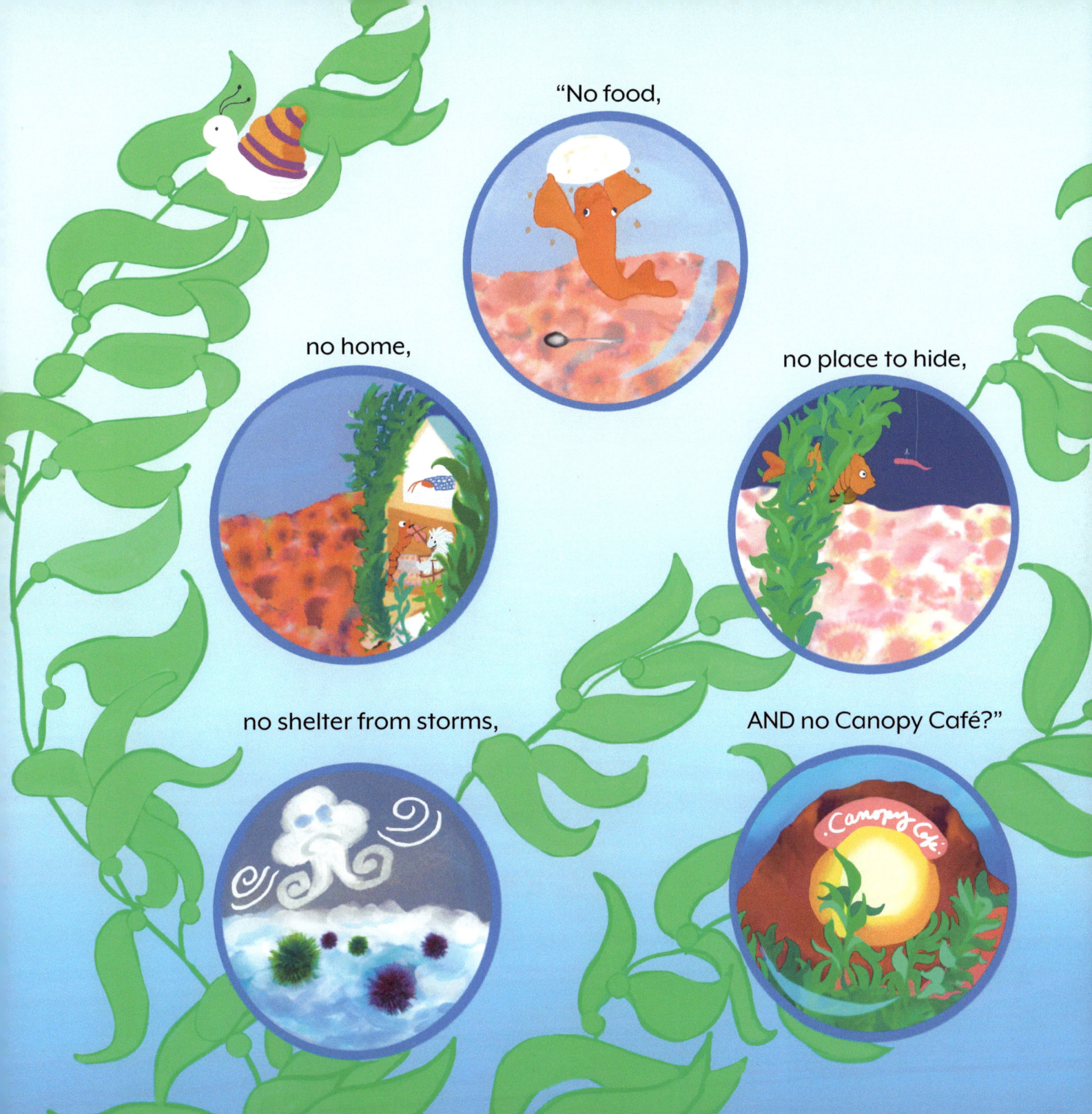

After lunch, Rudy swims to the top of the Kelp Forest for a breath of fresh air.

OOF! Something tugs at his ears, pulls at his nose, and scratches his paws and face. Something clutches his NECK! His heart pounds. Rudy is caught in a great big tangled mess!

He frantically yanks at some plastic gray thing, some rubbery red thing with a yellow string, some meshy green thing, and another thing that looks like it's holding water. The more he panics, the worse it gets! Finally, poor Rudy is completely pooped.

Rudy lies helpless at the surface of the sea, watching one urchin become two, then four, then more, and more, and more until they gather into an army. They munch on kelp, kelp, and more kelp, mowing down the forest as they march. Rudy feels so hungry.

Finally, Rudy hears a sweet sound rising from the depths.

His heart fills with hope as he sees his friends approaching.

"I can help!" shouts Opal. "I bet my rough radula tongue can cut through that suff if I try really hard."

"You?" says Rudy. "You're too small. We have no time to waste."

"Isaac the barber can help us," says Magda. "That crab has sharp claws. He'll snip through that stuff like he's clipping a mullet."

"I'm sorry," says Isaac. "I just molted. My claws are too soft. Can you wait a month for my shell to harden?"

Rudy's heart sinks. His neck hurts from the fur being rubbed off. There's no way he can wait a month. He feels Scout's fin on his shoulder.

"Let's try Valerie," she says.

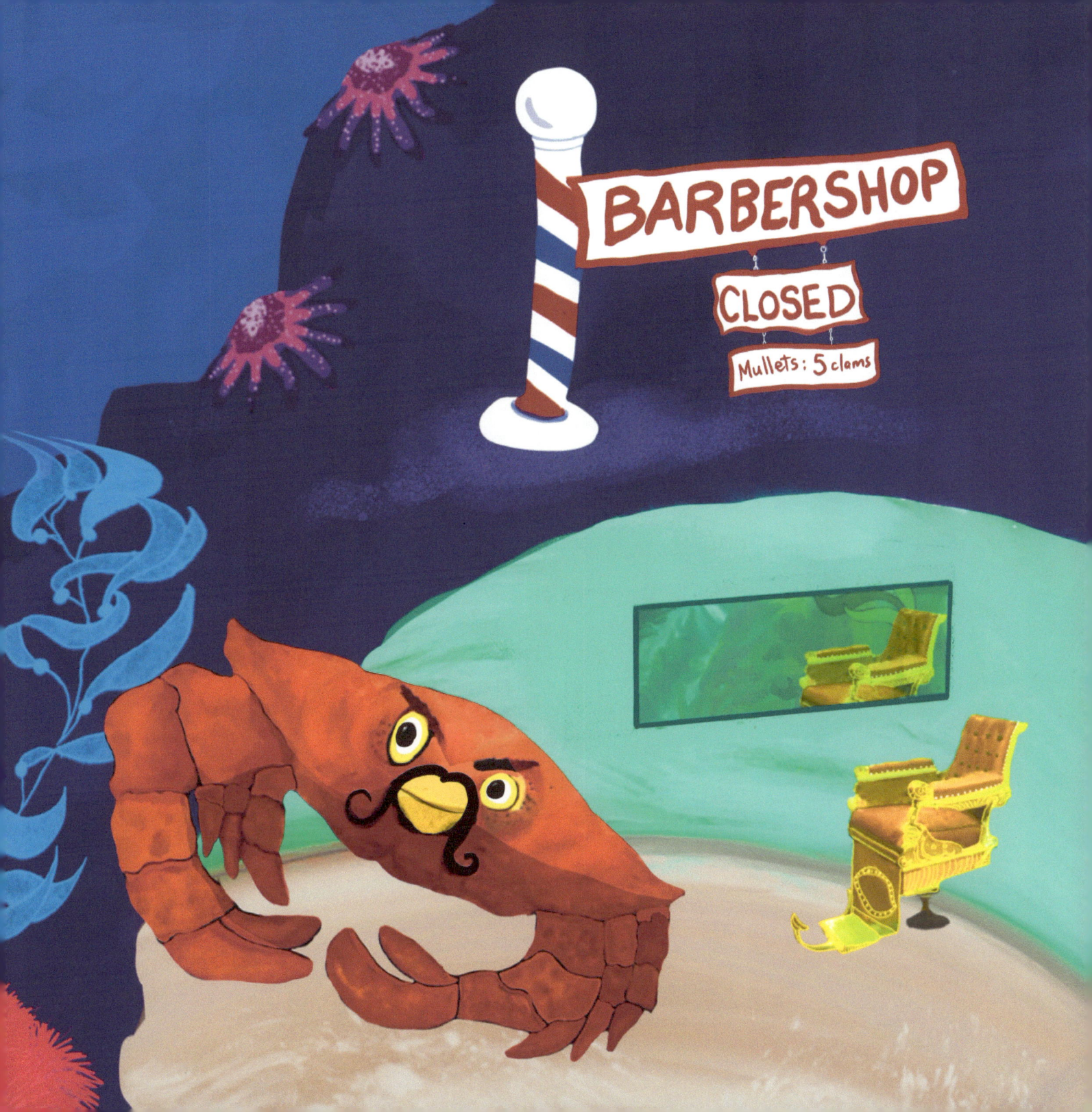

Valerie slips her tentacle into the mess of rubbish. She tugs, and she jerks, this way and that and finally gives it a good yank. But the mess of rubbish won't budge.

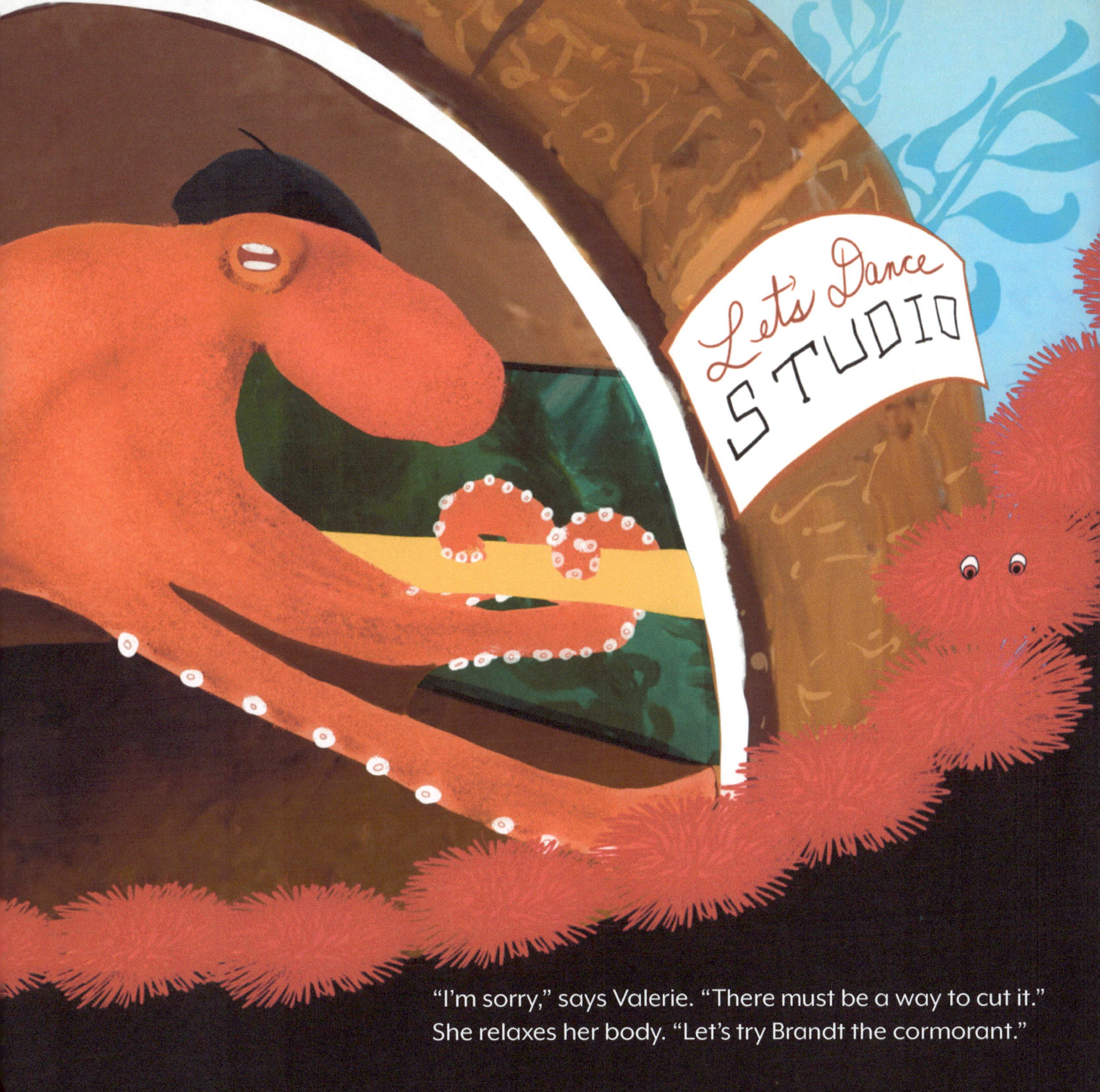

"I'm sorry," says Valerie. "There must be a way to cut it."
She relaxes her body. "Let's try Brandt the cormorant."

At Brandt's nesting island, a huge frothy surf stops them from getting any closer. A big wave lifts Rudy high enough for him to see Brandt sitting on his bird nest, helping his wife keep their eggs warm. Brandt does not see them or hear their cries.

Dominic is their last hope.

"Ah," hisses the shark. "I see you've brought me supper."

"NO, Dominic!" shouts Scout. "We need you to free Rudy from this tangled mess. Otherwise, there'll be nothing left for you to eat but prickly sea urchins."

"Well then…" Dominic pauses. "Luckily, I just ate lunch."

Rudy tries to be brave and hold still. The shark's jaws move closer. Rudy slips to the right.

As Dominic's teeth clamp shut, his front tooth breaks in half.

"Please take me home," Rudy whispers to Scout.

"It's hopeless," Rudy weeps.

His weeping turns to wailing.

His wailing turns to sobbing.

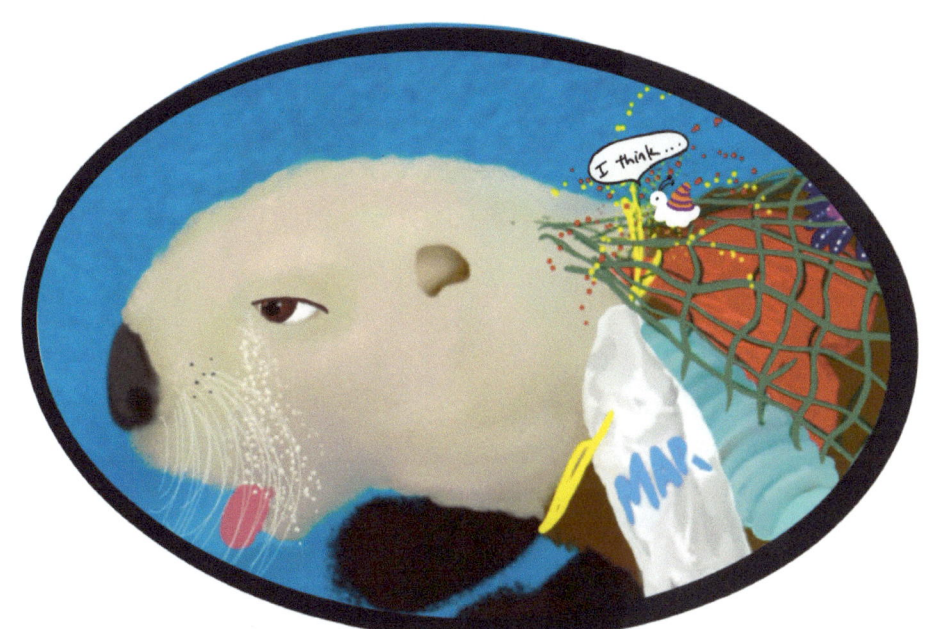

His sobbing turns to hiccups which grow bigger, and bigger, and bigger until...

Opal's radula cuts through!

The balloon, fishing net, water bottle, and shopping bag are all drifting away!

"Opal, is that you?" Rudy whispers hoarsely.

"It's me," says the snail. "I've been working really hard to help free you, Rudy!"

"I'm sorry I didn't believe in you, Opal," says Rudy.

"That's okay," says the snail. "I did!"

Everyone in the whole Kelp Forest sings at the top of their gills, "For She's a Jolly Good Snail!" even Dominic, cracked tooth and all. And then, after a long and merry celebration...

...Rudy and Opal settle in for a nice, long nap.

CPSIA information can be obtained
at www.ICGtesting.com
Printed in the USA
BVHW021536060722
641404BV00003B/7